GO TO BED!

* GO TO BED! *

A Book of Bedtime Poems

Selected by Lee Bennett Hopkins
Illustrated by Rosekrans Hoffman

Alfred A. Knopf  New York

For Jennifer who twinkles   L.B.H.

For Bob and Jim and Merlin   R.H.

This is a *Borzoi Book* published by Alfred A. Knopf, Inc.

Text Copyright © 1979 by Lee Bennett Hopkins. Illustrations Copyright © 1979 by Rosekrans Hoffman. All rights reserved under International and Pan-American Copyright Conventions. Published in the United States by Alfred A. Knopf, Inc., New York, and simultaneously in Canada by Random House of Canada Limited, Toronto. Distributed by Random House, Inc., New York. Manufactured in the United States of America
10 9 8 7 6 5 4 3 2 1

Library of Congress Cataloging in Publication Data

Go to bed! Summary: An anthology of poems depicting the pleasant and sometimes unpleasant aspects of bedtime. 1. Night—Juvenile poetry. 2. Sleep—Juvenile poetry. [1. Night—Poetry. 2. Sleep—Poetry] I. Hopkins, Lee Bennett. II. Hoffman, Rosekrans. PN6110.C4G658 811'.008 78-3575 ISBN 0-394-83869-6 ISBN 0-394-93869-0 lib. bdg.

✱ Acknowledgments

Every effort has been made to trace the ownership of all copyrighted material and to secure the necessary permissions to reprint these selections. In the event of any question arising as to the use of any material, the editor and the publisher, while expressing regret for any inadvertent error, will be happy to make the necessary correction in future printings.

Thanks are due to the following for permission to reprint the copyrighted material listed below:

Atheneum Publishers, Inc. for "It is always" from GOODBYE, YESTERDAY: A Book of Poems by Joan Walsh Anglund. Copyright © 1974 by Joan Walsh Anglund.

The Bobbs-Merrill Co., Inc. for "Charlie's Bedtime" by Lee Bennett Hopkins from CHARLIE'S WORLD. Copyright © 1972 by Lee Bennett Hopkins.

Curtis Brown, Ltd. for "In the Pitch of the Night" by Lee Bennett Hopkins. Copyright © 1978 by Lee Bennett Hopkins.

E.P. Dutton & Co., Inc. for "Going to Bed" by Marchette Chute from AROUND AND AROUND by Marchette Chute. Copyright © 1957 by E.P. Dutton.

Harcourt, Brace Jovanovich, Inc. for "Keep A Poem in Your Pocket" by Beatrice Schenk de Regniers from SOMETHING SPECIAL. Copyright © 1958 by Beatrice Schenk de Regniers; "My Star" by Myra Cohn Livingston from THE MOON AND A STAR. Copyright © 1965 by Myra Cohn Livingston.

Harper & Row, Publishers, Inc. for an extract from THE BED BOOK by Sylvia Plath, pictures by Emily Arnold McCully. Text copyright © 1976 by Ted Hughes; "In the Middle of the Night" by Karla Kuskin from IN THE MIDDLE OF THE TREES by Karla Kuskin. Copyright © 1958 by Karla Kuskin; "Pete at the Zoo" by Gwendolyn Brooks from THE WORLD OF GWENDOLYN BROOKS. Copyright © 1960 by Gwendolyn Brooks.

Margaret Hillert for "My Teddy Bear." Used by permission of the author who controls all rights.

* Contents

GO TO BED!

Keep a Poem in Your Pocket

Keep a poem in your pocket
and a picture in your head
and you'll never feel lonely
at night when you're in bed.

The little poem will sing to you
the little picture bring to you
a dozen dreams to dance to you
at night when you're in bed.

So—
Keep a picture in your pocket
and a poem in your head
and you'll never feel lonely
at night when you're in bed.

Beatrice Schenk de Regniers

3

FROM

The Bed Book

These are the Beds
to climb into:

Pocket-size Beds
and Beds for Snacks,
Tank Beds, Beds
on Elephant Backs,
Beds that fly,
or go under water,
Bouncy Beds, Beds
you can spatter and spotter,
Bird-Watching Beds,
Beds for Zero Weather—
any kind of Bed
as long as it's rather
special and queer
and full of surprises,

Beds of amazing
shapes and sizes—

NOT just a white little
tucked-in-tight little
nighty-night little
turn-out-the-light little
    bed!

Sylvia Plath

5

Going to Bed

I'm always told to hurry up—
    Which I'd be glad to do,
If there were not so many things
    That need attending to.

But first I have to find my towel
    Which fell behind the rack,
And when a pillow's thrown at me
    I have to throw it back.

And then I have to get the things
    I need in bed with me.
Like marbles and my birthday train
    And Pete the chimpanzee.

6

I have to see my polliwog
   Is safely in its pan,
And stand a minute on my head
   To be quite sure I can.

I have to bounce upon my bed
   To see if it will sink,
And then when I am covered up
   I find a need a drink.

Marchette Chute

7

Bedtime

Five minutes, five minutes more, please!
  Let me stay five minutes more!
Can't I just finish the castle
  I'm building here on the floor?
Can't I just finish the story
  I'm reading here in my book?
Can't I just finish this bead-chain—
  It **almost** is finished, look!
Can't I just finish this game, please?
  When a game's once begun
It's a pity never to find out
  Whether you've lost or won.
Can't I just stay five minutes?
  Well, can't I stay just four?
Three minutes, then? two minutes?
  Can't I stay **one** minute more?

Eleanor Farjeon

8

Charlie's Bedtime

Can you bring me a glass of water?
Can I have a little juice?
Can I say goodnight to Daddy again?
Will you read me Dr. Seuss?

Will I see you in the morning, Mommy?
Can I keep on the light?

Oh—
If only I'd find a real way
To chase away the night.

Lee Bennett Hopkins

9

Night Comes...

Night comes
leaking
out of the sky.

Stars come
peeking.

Moon comes
sneaking,
silvery-sly.

Who is
shaking,
shivery-
quaking?

Who is afraid
of the night?

Not I.

Beatrice Schenk de Regniers

My Star

My star comes out
When I'm in bed.
    There is a place to put my head
    where I can watch it twinkle
    high
    in one small windowpane of sky.

Myra Cohn Livingston

11

Things to Do if You Are a Star

Twinkle
and
Twinkle
and
Twinkle
and
Twinkle
and
Twinkle

Bobbi Katz

12

FROM
How Shall I Fly to the Moon?

Why can't I bring home a star
    for you, Mother?
Why can't I bring home a star?
    Because stars in the sky are for
        wishing upon,
    The stars are meant only for
        wishing on, son,
    The stars are for wishing upon.

Gail Kredenser

13

My Teddy Bear

A teddy bear is nice to hold.
The one I have is getting old.
His paws are almost wearing out
And so's his funny furry snout
From rubbing on my nose of skin,
And all his fur is pretty thin.
A ribbon and a piece of string
Make a sort of necktie thing.
His eyes came out and now instead
He has some new ones made of thread.
I take him everywhere I go
And tell him all the things I know.
I like the way he feels at night,
All snuggled up against me tight.

Margaret Hillert

14

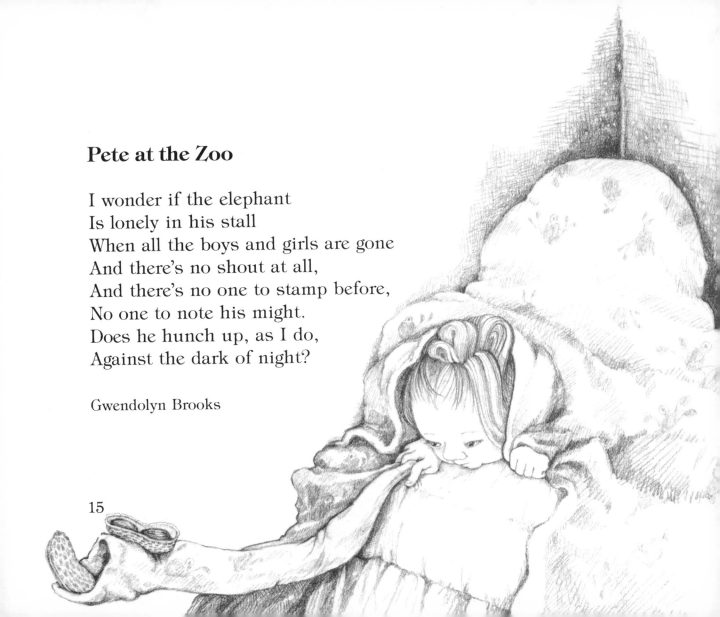

Pete at the Zoo

I wonder if the elephant
Is lonely in his stall
When all the boys and girls are gone
And there's no shout at all,
And there's no one to stamp before,
No one to note his might.
Does he hunch up, as I do,
Against the dark of night?

Gwendolyn Brooks

15

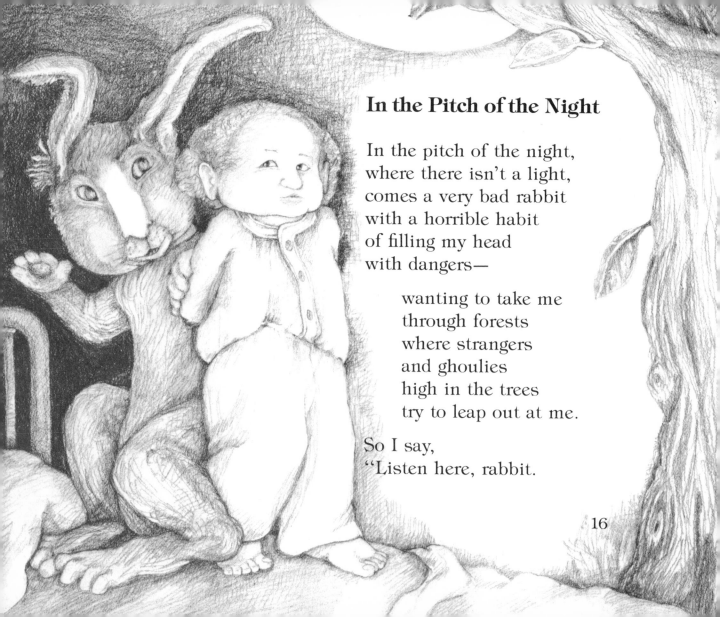

In the Pitch of the Night

In the pitch of the night,
where there isn't a light,
comes a very bad rabbit
with a horrible habit
of filling my head
with dangers—

    wanting to take me
    through forests
    where strangers
    and ghoulies
    high in the trees
    try to leap out at me.

So I say,
"Listen here, rabbit.

16

I'm sick of your habit.
I've had enough
of your nightmarish fright.

My bed is **my** bed
not some rabbit-filled head

    of monsters and dragons
    and weird plants that bite!

Now get out of my room!
Go on your own way!
Sleep has to come
before
    night
       turns
          to
            day!''

Lee Bennett Hopkins

In Bed

When I am in bed
I hear
footsteps of the night
sharp
like the crackling of a dead leaf
in the stillness.

Then my mother laughs
downstairs.

Charlotte Zolotow

18

Now I Lay Me Down

Now I lay me down to sleep,
I pray thee Lord, my soul to keep;
Thy love stay with me through the night
And wake me with the morning light.
                    Amen.

Anonymous

19

The Middle of the Night

This is a song to be sung at night
When nothing is left of you and the light
When the cats don't bark
And the mice don't moo
And the nightmares come and nuzzle you
When there's blackness in the cupboards
And the closet and the hall
And a tipping, tapping, rapping
In the middle of the wall
When the lights have one by one gone out
All over everywhere
And a shadow by the curtains
Bumps a shadow by the chair
Then you hide beneath your pillow
With your eyes shut very tight
And you sing

"There's nothing sweeter than
The middle of the night.
I'm extremely fond of shadows
And I really must confess
That cats and bats don't scare me
Well, they couldn't scare me less
And most of all I like the things
That slide and slip and creep."
It really is surprising
How fast you fall asleep.

Karla Kuskin

The Dream Keeper

Bring me all of your dreams,
You dreamers,
Bring me all of your
Heart melodies
That I may wrap them
In a blue cloud-cloth
Away from the too-rough fingers
Of the world.

Langston Hughes

22

How Far?

How far is a dream?
    As far as a star
    High in the sky?

How far is a dream?
    At the close of the day
    A dream is just
    A pillow away.

Leland B. Jacobs

23

The Land of Nod

From breakfast on through all the day
At home among my friends I stay;
But every night I go abroad
Afar into the land of Nod.

All by myself I have to go.
With none to tell me what to do—
All alone beside the streams
And up the mountain-sides of dreams.

The strangest things are there for me,
Both things to eat and things to see,
And many frightening sights abroad
Till morning in the land of Nod.

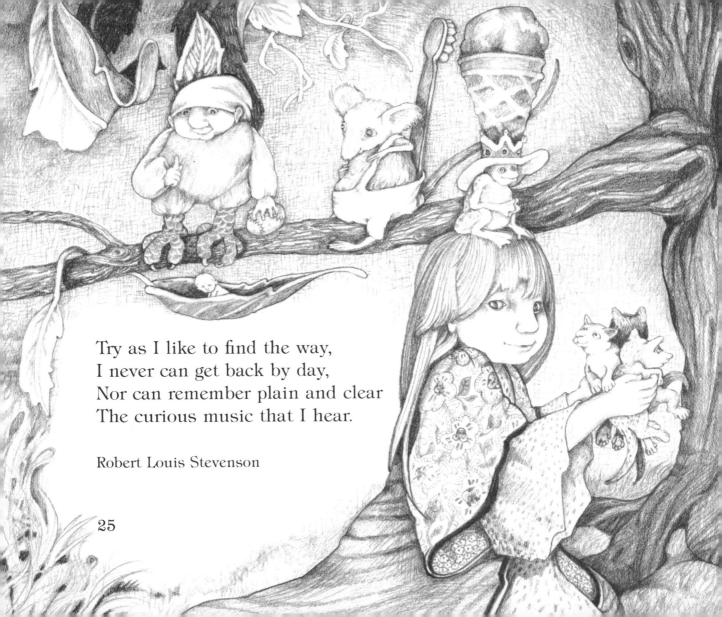

Try as I like to find the way,
I never can get back by day,
Nor can remember plain and clear
The curious music that I hear.

Robert Louis Stevenson

25

A Dream…

A dream
Is wonderful
There are good and bad dreams
A dream lets you go to Never-
Land Land.

Jody Duerr

26

It Is Always...

It is always
   Tomorrow
      somewhere.

A new day
   is forever
      beginning.

Joan Walsh Anglund

27

✱ **Lee Bennett Hopkins** is the editor of a number of highly acclaimed poetry anthologies among them ON OUR WAY: POEMS OF PRIDE AND LOVE, and the ALA Notable, DON'T YOU TURN BACK: POEMS BY LANGSTON HUGHES. His fiction for young people includes I LOVED ROSE ANN and MAMA (all published by Knopf). A member of the Board of Directors for the National Council of Teachers of English, he chaired the 1978 Poetry Award Committee.

Mr. Hopkins lives in Scarborough, New York.

✱ **Rosekrans Hoffman's** distinctive talents as a children's book illustrator can be seen in such outstanding titles as ALEXANDRA THE ROCK-EATER, and ANNA BANANA which she both wrote and illustrated for Knopf, as well as a number of other captivating picturebooks. A painter turned illustrator, her works have been exhibited at several museums including the Whitney Museum and the Brooklyn Museum.

Ms. Hoffman lives in West Haven, Connecticut.